Giraffes

Laura Marsh

NATIONAL
GEOGRAPHIC

Washington, D.C.

For Eileen, Children's Librarian at the Scarsdale Library —L. F. M.

Trade paperback ISBN: 978-1-4263-2448-2
Reinforced library binding ISBN: 978-1-4263-2449-9

The publisher and author gratefully acknowledge the expert content review of this book by Katie Ahl, Woodland Park Zoo, and the literacy review of this book by Mariam Jean Dreher, professor of reading education, University of Maryland, College Park.

Art Director: Amanda Larsen
Designer: YAY! Design

Photo Credits
COVER (Front), Richard Du Toit/Minden Pictures; 1 (CTR), Michael Poliza/National Geographic Creative; 3 (LO RT), RJ08/Shutterstock; 4-5 (LE), Sherrod Photography/Shutterstock; 6 (CTR), drpnncpptak/Shutterstock; 6 (RT), GlobalStock/Getty Images; 7 (LO), Photoshot License Ltd/ Alamy; 8 (UP), Frans Lanting/Science Source; 8 (CTR), Anup Shah/Nature Picture Library; 8 (LO), David Hosking/Minden Pictures; 9 (LO), Steven Ruiter/Minden Pictures; 10-11 (UP), John Warburton-Lee Photography/Alamy; 12-13 (CTR), Wayne Hughes/Alamy; 13 (UP RT), feelphoto/ Shutterstock; 14 (CTR), georgesanker.com/ Alamy; 15 (CTR), Richard Du Toit/Minden Pictures; 16-17 (CTR), Panoramic Images/Getty Images; 18 (UP LE), Martin Harvey/Kimball Stock; 18 (CTR), Mitsuaki Iwago/Minden Pictures; 18 (LO LE), meunierd/Shutterstock; 19 (UP LE), joSon/Getty Images; 19 (CTR RT), Daniel J. Cox/ Kimball Stock; 19 (LO LE), Terry Andrewartha/ Minden Pictures; 20 (CTR), Stephan Bonneau/ Minden Pictures; 21 (UP), Barcroft Media/Getty Images; 22 (CTR), Stacey Ann Alberts/Shutter- stock; 24 (UP), Horst Klemm/Great Stock/Corbis; 24 (LO), Jim Brandenburg/Minden Pictures; 26 (UP), Stephen Belcher/Corbis; 27 (CTR), Lou Coetzer/Nature Picture Library; 28 (CTR), All Canada Photos/Alamy; 29 (CTR), Mitsuyoshi Tatematsu/Minden Pictures; 30 (LO LE), Pictures Wild/Shutterstock; 30 (LO RT), moizhusein/ Shutterstock; 31 (UP LE), Hanne & Jens Eriksen/ Nature Picture Library; 31 (UP RT), PhotoDisc; 31 (LO LE), Jak Wonderly/National Geographic; 31 (LO RT), schankz/Shutterstock; 32 (UP LE), Denis-Huot/Nature Picture Library; 32 (UP RT), Photodisc; 32 (LO LE), John Warburton-Lee Photography/Alamy; 32 (LO RT), Jim Branden- burg/Minden Pictures; Top border (throughout), Photomario/Shutterstock; Vocabulary box art (throughout), Danilo Sanino/Shutterstock

National Geographic supports K–12 educators with ELA Common Core Resources. Visit natgeoed.org/commoncore for more information.

Printed in the United States of America
16/WOR/1

Table of Contents

Guess Who! 4

Big Bodies 6

Giraffes at Home 10

Mealtime 12

6 Fun Facts About Giraffes 18

Big Babies 20

On the Lookout 24

Nap Time 28

What in the World? 30

Glossary 32

Guess Who!

What do you call an animal so tall, it reaches the treetops with no help at all?

That's a big clue. Do you want to guess who?

A giraffe!

Big Bodies

Did you know that giraffes are the tallest animals on land?

Their legs are as tall as a grown man. Their necks are just as tall. If you add in their bodies, that means giraffes can be 14 to 19 feet tall!

Giraffes are much taller than other animals.

Giraffes have spots. Their spots can be light tan. They can also be brown or almost black.

How are the giraffes' patterns different?

Each giraffe has a pattern of spots. But no two giraffes have the same pattern. That's how you can tell them apart.

Word Spot

PATTERN: A collection of shapes that makes a design

Giraffes at Home

A herd of giraffes walks on the African plains.

Giraffes live where it's hot and dry. They live on the plains in Africa (AF-rih-kuh).

Word Spot

PLAINS: An area of land that is flat and wide with a few trees

Giraffes stay together in a group. The group is called a herd. A herd usually has six to twelve giraffes.

Mealtime

For giraffes, it's always mealtime!

They eat for 16 to 20 hours every day. That means they eat lots and lots of leaves.

These giraffes have stopped to eat from acacia trees.

Most of these leaves are from acacia (uh-KAY-shuh) trees.

A giraffe can reach leaves that other animals can't get.

A giraffe's body helps it get food. A long neck helps a giraffe get leaves up high.

A long tongue and wide lips grab leaves. These body parts work together to reach around thorns.

A giraffe's body can also get in the way. Giraffes have to bend way down to get a drink.

But the acacia leaves they eat have lots of water in them. So giraffes only need to drink every few days.

17

6 FUN FACTS
About Giraffes

1 A giraffe's tongue is blue-black up front and pink on the back. The dark color helps keep the tongue from getting a sunburn!

A baby giraffe can run a few hours after it's born.

2

3 Male giraffes are called bulls. Females are called cows.

4

A large male giraffe can weigh up to 3,000 pounds.

If a giraffe eats a thorn, not to worry! Giraffes have thick saliva, or spit, that will coat any thorns that are eaten.

5

6

A giraffe has two horns on its head. Males use them to fight with other males.

Big Babies

At birth, a calf weighs as much as an adult human woman.

Some big animals have small babies. But not giraffes. They are big animals that have big babies.

A baby giraffe weighs 100 to 150 pounds when it's born. It is called a calf.

Young giraffes
stay with other
calves during
the day.

A mother in the herd babysits. This helps keep the calves safe. The other adults leave to look for food.

On the Lookout

Nile crocodile

Adult giraffes also look out for each other. They watch for predators (PRED-uh-ters) like lions and crocodiles.

If a giraffe sees a predator, it snorts. This warns the others: Run!

Giraffes can run very fast for a short time. This helps them get away.

Hard hooves can keep a lion away.

They can use their hooves
to kick a predator, too.

Word Spot

HOOVES: The hard covering on the feet of some animals

Nap Time

All that watching and eating doesn't leave much time for sleep. Luckily, giraffes need less than three hours of sleep every day.

They usually nap standing
up. But not always!

What in the World?

These pictures are close-up views of things in a giraffe's world. Use the hints to figure out what's in the pictures. Answers are on page 31.

1

HINT: They can be used to kick.

2

HINT: A giraffe's home is here.

Word Bank

spots   tongue   leaves   horns   hooves   plains

3

HINT: Giraffes eat lots of these.

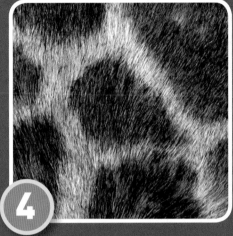

4

HINT: These make a pattern.

5

HINT: A giraffe has one that is long and dark.

6

HINT: A giraffe's head has two.

Answers: 1. hooves, 2. plains, 3. leaves, 4. spots, 5. tongue, 6. horns

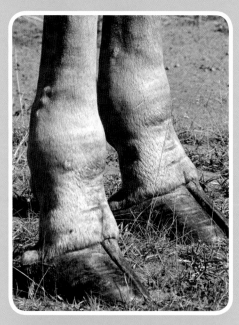

HOOVES: The hard covering on the feet of some animals

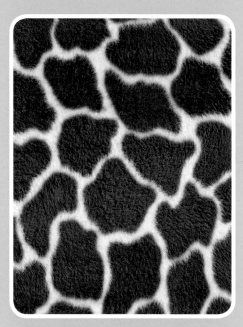

PATTERN: A collection of shapes that makes a design

PLAINS: An area of land that is flat and wide with a few trees

PREDATOR: An animal that hunts other animals for food